LIGHTNING
BOLT
BOOKS™

How Do Computers Talk to One Another?

Melissa Abramovitz

Lerner Publications • Minneapolis

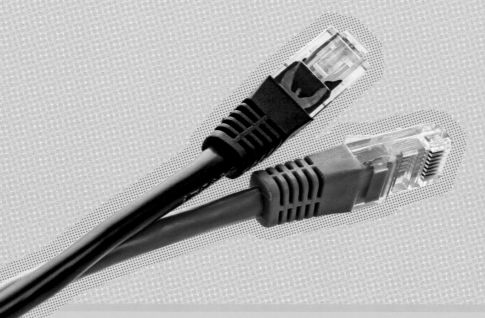

Content Consultant: John Sartori, Assistant Professor, Electrical and Computer Engineering, University of Minnesota

Lerner Publications Company
A division of Lerner Publishing Group, Inc.
241 First Avenue North
Minneapolis, MN 55401 USA

For reading levels and more information, look up this title at www.lernerbooks.com.

Library of Congress Cataloging-in-Publication Data

Abramovitz, Melissa, 1954-
    How do computers talk to one another? / by Melissa Abramovitz.
        pages   cm. — (Lightning bolt books. Our digital world)
    Includes bibliographical references and index.
    Audience: 5-8.
    Audience: K to grade 3.
    ISBN 978-1-4677-8075-9 (lb : alk. paper) — ISBN 978-1-4677-8317-0 (pb : alk. paper) —
ISBN 978-1-4677-8318-7 (eb pdf)
    1. Computer networks—Juvenile literature. 2. Wireless Internet—Juvenile literature.
3. Computers—Juvenile literature. I. Title.
TK5105.5.A243 2015
004.6—dc23   2015000427

Manufactured in the United States of America
1 – BP – 7/15/15

Table of Contents

What Are Computer Networks?

Computers connect to share information. A group of connected computers is called a computer network.

Most of the computers you use are part of networks.

Have you ever sent an e-mail to your grandma? Have you played a game online? Have you watched funny videos on the Internet? Then you have used a computer network.

E-mails travel over computer networks.

Many devices in one home can connect to a network.

Some computer networks are small. They connect computers within one home. They let families share music, photos, and more.

The largest
computer network
is the Internet.
It connects billions of
computers around
the world.

This machine was used to build an early computer network.

The Internet was created in the 1960s. The US government connected its computers together. It wanted to share information quickly and safely.

Most US households are connected to the Internet.

In the 1980s, many people connected to the Internet. By 1995, it became very popular. These days, nearly everyone in the United States is online.

Connecting to the Internet

You cannot get online by yourself. You need the help of an Internet service provider (ISP). These companies run cables through cities and towns.

Many Internet cables run underground.

The cables connect to form a computer network.

They branch through neighborhoods. They go to each home.

Workers run networking cables from home to home.

Some cables are
made of copper.

This material can carry
information as electrical signals.

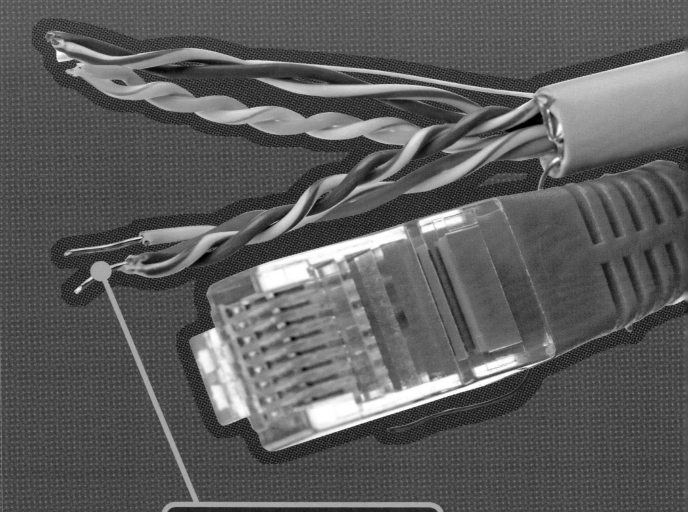

Copper cables have
plastic around them
for protection.

Newer cables are made of glass. They are known as fiber-optic cables. They can carry more information than copper. But they are also more expensive.

Fiber-optic cables contain many thin pieces of glass.

Customers pay ISPs to connect to the Internet.

Most customers pay an ISP every month for a home Internet connection.

Faster connections are more expensive. They let users send and receive lots of data quickly. Websites load more quickly on a fast connection.

You need a fast connection to watch videos from websites such as YouTube.

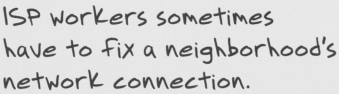

ISP workers sometimes have to fix a neighborhood's network connection.

Each ISP connects many computers together. They form a network.

When ISPs join their networks together, they make up the Internet.

ISPs use devices called switches to connect to one another.

Packets of Information

Packet   Packet   Packet

Computers turn photos and other information into many small chunks called packets. Breaking information into packets allows it to be sent across the Internet.

Each packet has two parts. The first is called user data. User data is the photo, the e-mail, or other information you are sending. The second is called control information. Control information says where the packet came from. It also says where it is going.

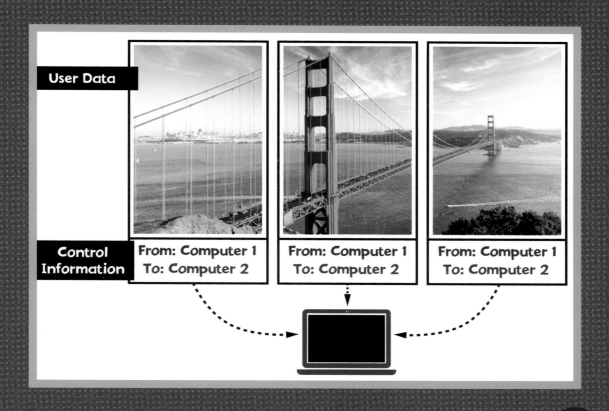

| User Data | | | |
| Control Information | From: Computer 1 To: Computer 2 | From: Computer 1 To: Computer 2 | From: Computer 1 To: Computer 2 |

Lights on this modem show when packets are coming or going.

A modem turns the packets into electrical signals. It sends these signals onto the network.

The modem also receives electrical signals.

It turns them back into packets. The computer puts the packets together. It rebuilds the user data.

Packets do not travel directly to where they are going. They bounce between devices on the network. These devices are called routers. Routers choose the route a packet should take.

Small routers send packets through a home network.

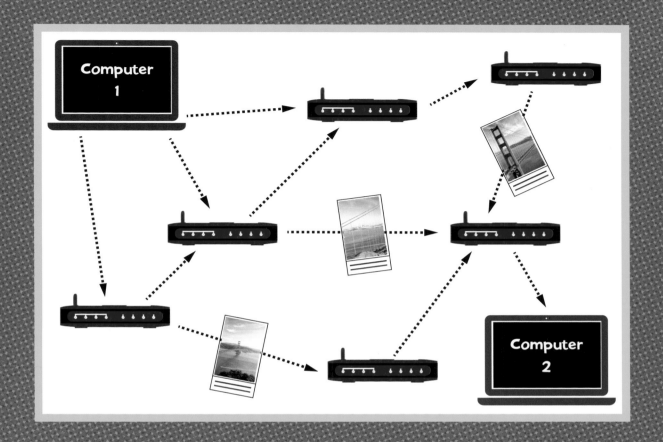

Packets travel from router to router. They keep moving until they reach the place they are meant to go to. Different packets from a single e-mail may take different paths. They end up together in the end.

Wireless Networks

Not all computers sit on desks and have big screens. Smartphones are computers too.

How do smartphones connect to the Internet?

People listen to online music on smartphones. How do the music packets get to your phone?

Cell phone towers can send packets to phones many miles away.

Cell phone companies set up towers. These towers are connected to an ISP. The towers send out packets in radio waves. The packets travel through the air. Smartphones turn the radio waves back into packets.

Smartphones also send packets back to the tower using an antenna. This can connect you to a friend who lives far away. Computer networks are an important part of our world. They help people all around the planet stay connected.

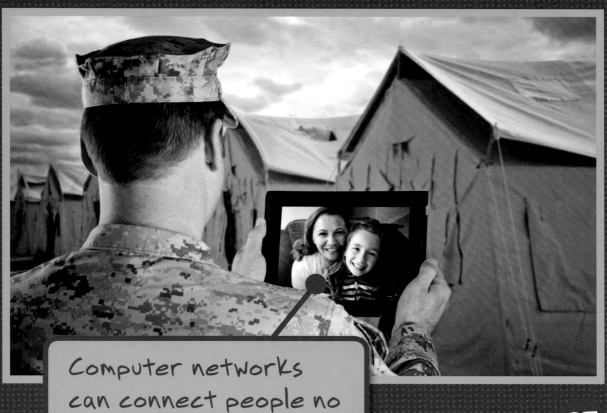

Computer networks can connect people no matter where they are.

Takeaway Tips

- To see packets in action, visit any website. A faraway computer broke the website into packets. The packets traveled over the Internet through many paths. Your computer turned them back into the website you see on your screen.

- Remember that any connection between computers is a network. Two computers in your home can connect to form a network. So can billions of computers on the Internet.

- A smartphone antenna uses a lot of energy. You can turn off your phone's antenna to make your battery last longer. Most phones let you do this.

Fun Facts

- **Computer scientist Ray Tomlinson sent the first e-mail in 1971.**

- **Fiber-optic cables are made of glass strands as thin as a human hair.**

- **More than 2.4 billion people around the world use the Internet.**

- **In the 1990s, people's homes often used the same cables for phones and the Internet. When you wanted to go online, you had to make sure no one was using the phone.**

Glossary

antenna: a device that sends and receives radio waves

cable: a bundle of wires

data: information

modem: a device that changes computer data into electrical signals and back again. These signals can be sent through computer networks.

network: a group of connected computers

packet: a small chunk of computer data

router: a device that chooses the path that packets will take through a computer network

Further Reading

Boothroyd, Jennifer. *From Typewriters to Text Messages: How Communication Has Changed.* Minneapolis: Lerner Publications, 2012.

Greve, Meg. *The Internet.* Vero Beach, FL: Rourke Educational Media, 2014.

How Does the Internet Work? http://computer.howstuffworks.com/internet/basics/internet.htm

Owings, Lisa. *Stay Safe Online.* Minneapolis: Lerner Publications, 2014.

Swanson, Jennifer. *How the Internet Works.* Mankato, MN: Child's World, 2012.

Index

Photo Acknowledgments

The images in this book are used with the permission of: © samsonovs/Shutterstock
Images, p. 2; © Ronnachai Palas/Shutterstock Images, p. 4; © Firma V/Shutterstock
Images, p. 5; © Squaredpixels/iStockphoto, p. 6; © Anton Balazh/Shutterstock Images,
p. 7; © Fred Prouser/Reuters/Corbis, p. 8; © szefei/Shutterstock Images, p. 9;
© ChiccoDodiFC/Shutterstock Images, p. 10; © Ariana Lindquist/Bloomberg/Getty
Images, p. 11; © ra3rn/Shutterstock Images, p. 12; © zentilia/iStock/Thinkstock, p. 13;
© Cheryl Savan/Shutterstock Images, p. 14; © Bloomua/Shutterstock Images, p. 15;
© kadmy/iStockphoto, p. 16; © dotshock/Shutterstock Images, p. 17; © somchaij/
iStockphoto, pp. 18, 19, 23; © koosen/iStockphoto, p. 20; © KPG Payless2/Shutterstock
Images, p. 21; © fotoslaz/Shutterstock Images, p. 22; © Oleksiy Mark/Shutterstock
Images, p. 24; © George Muresan/Shutterstock Images, p. 25; © jakelv7500/
Shutterstock Images, p. 26; © Straight 8 Photography/Shutterstock Images, p. 27;
© Andrey Popov/Shutterstock Images, p. 28; © Eugene Shapovalov/Shutterstock
Images, p. 30; © Hasloo Group Production Studio/Shutterstock Images, p. 31.

Front cover: © Todd Strand/Independent Picture Service; © Rose Braverman/flickr
.com, (Palm Trees Background) (CC BY 2.0); PhotoDisc Royalty Free by Getty, (Mountain
Lion Background).

Main body text set in Johann Light 30/36.